THE SUN

KATE RIGGS

Creative Education · Creative Paperbacks

Published by Creative Education and Creative Paperbacks
P.O. Box 227, Mankato, Minnesota 56002
Creative Education and Creative Paperbacks are imprints of
The Creative Company
www.thecreativecompany.us

Design and production by Chelsey Luther
Printed in the United States of America

Photographs by Corbis (Ken Crawford/Stocktrek Images, Tomasz Dabrowski/
Stocktrek Images, Mark Garlick/Science Photo Library, Mehau Kulyk/Science
Photo Library, Mark Garlick Words & Pictures Ltd/Science Photo Library, Mitsushi
Okada/amanaimages, Detlev van Ravenswaay/Science Photo Library), deviantART
(AlmightyHighElf), Dreamstime (Mopic, Oriontrail), Getty Images (Detlev van
Ravenswaay, Stocktrek Images), NASA (NASA/ESA/J. Hester [ASU], NASA/
ESA/Hubble SM4 ERO Team, NASA/JPL-Caltech/STScI), Science Source (John
Chumack, Mark Garlick, Paul Wootton), Shutterstock (jupeart)

Library of Congress Cataloging-in-Publication Data
Riggs, Kate.
The sun / Kate Riggs.
p. cm. — (Across the universe)
Summary: A young scientist's guide to the sun and other stars, including how
they interact with other elements in the universe and emphasizing how questions
and observations can lead to discovery.
Includes bibliographical references and index.
ISBN 978-1-60818-485-9 (hardcover)
ISBN 978-1-62832-085-5 (pbk)
1. Sun—Juvenile literature. I. Title.
QB521.5.R54 2015
523.7—dc23   2014002294

CCSS: RI.1.1, 2, 3, 4, 5, 6, 7; RI.2.1, 2, 3, 5, 6, 7, 10;
RI.3.1, 3, 5, 7, 8; RF.2.3, 4; RF.3.3

First Edition
9 8 7 6 5 4 3 2 1

Pages 20–21 "Astronomy at Home"
activity instructions adapted from
from the Center for Science
Education at UC Berkeley:
http://cse.ssl.berkeley.edu
/AtHomeAstronomy/activity_02.html

TABLE OF CONTENTS

Did you know that the sun is a star? Scientists called astronomers study the sun. The **planets** in our **solar system** orbit, or go around, the sun. Other stars in the **galaxy** shine brightly. But they are not as close as the sun. They are so far away that we cannot see them moving.

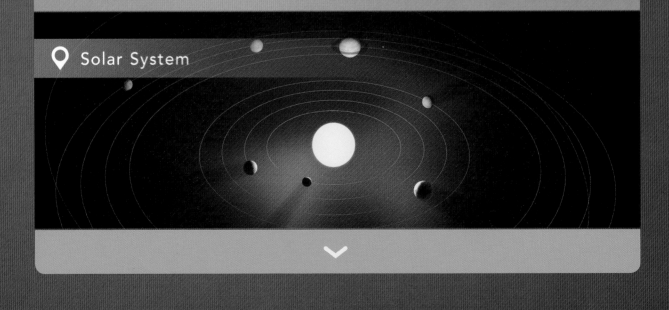

📍 Solar System

The closest star after the sun is named Proxima Centauri.

Distance between stars is measured in light years. A light year is how far light travels in one year. It is equal to about 6 trillion miles (9.5 trillion km)! Proxima Centauri is about 4.2 light years away from Earth.

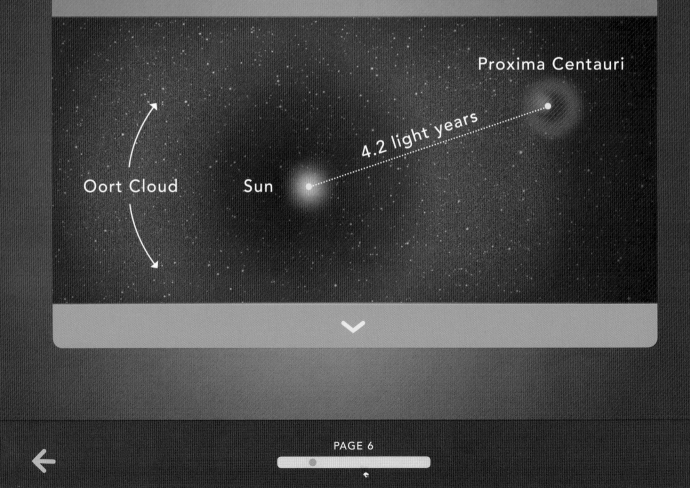

Proxima Centauri

4.2 light years

Oort Cloud

Sun

The sun is about 93 million miles (150 million km) away from Earth.

Earth

The sun and other stars are balls of burning gases. Supernovas are stars that get brighter and brighter. Then they explode! A star can live for billions of years. Our sun will probably be around for another 5 billion years.

Supernovas form out of stars that are bigger than the sun.

When the sun dies,
it will get bigger
and closer to Earth.

Rigel is a blue supergiant that is 25 times bigger than the sun.

>

Astronomers group stars by color and temperature. Red stars are the coldest stars. Blue stars are the hottest. The sun is a yellow star. It is warmer and larger than red stars. But it is colder and smaller than blue stars.

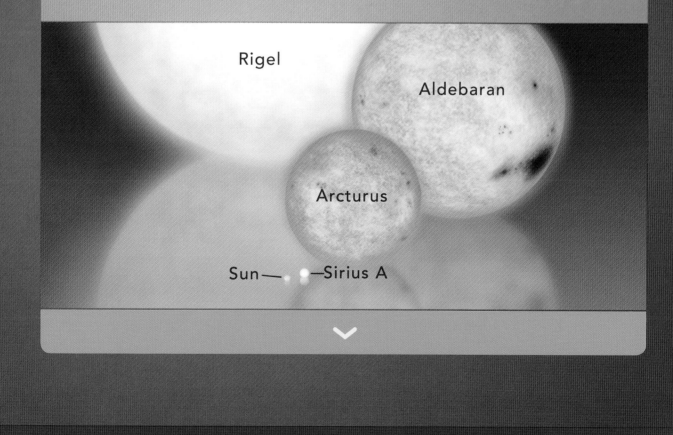

Rigel

Aldebaran

Arcturus

Sun — Sirius A

The sun will turn into a red giant someday. It will get bigger and cooler. The brightest red giant we can see is named Arcturus. It is 36.7 light years away. It looks like the fourth-brightest star in the sky.

Arcturus is a name that means "Bear Watcher."

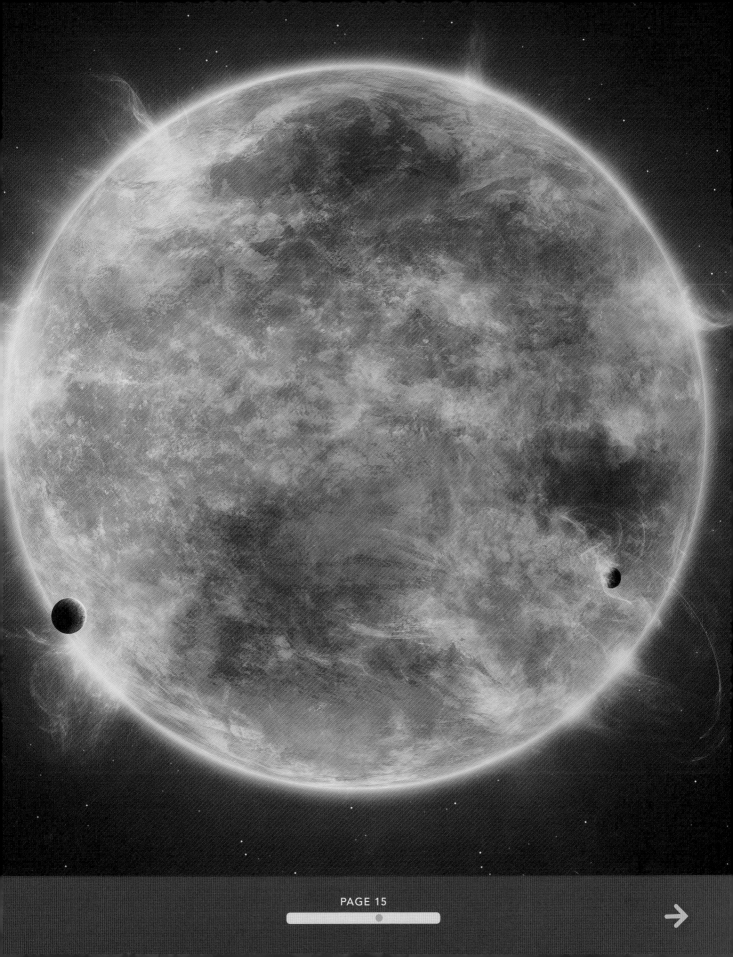

Life on Earth is possible because of the sun. It gives us heat and light. It makes the seasons change. The sun's **gravity** keeps the planets spinning around it.

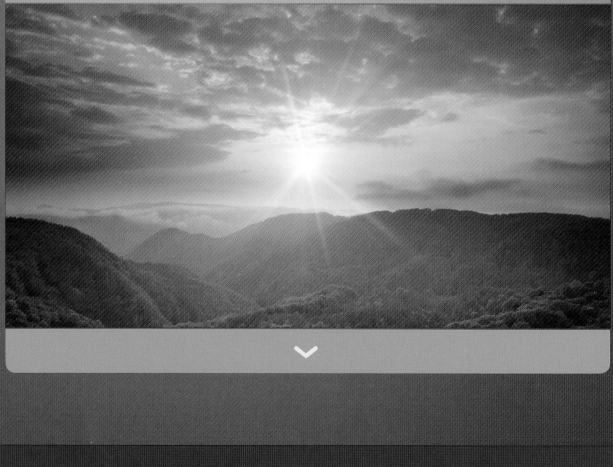

The sun's core, or center, is about 27,000,000 °F (15,000,000 °C).

Earth

Tell someone what you know about the sun! What else can you discover?

coronal streamer

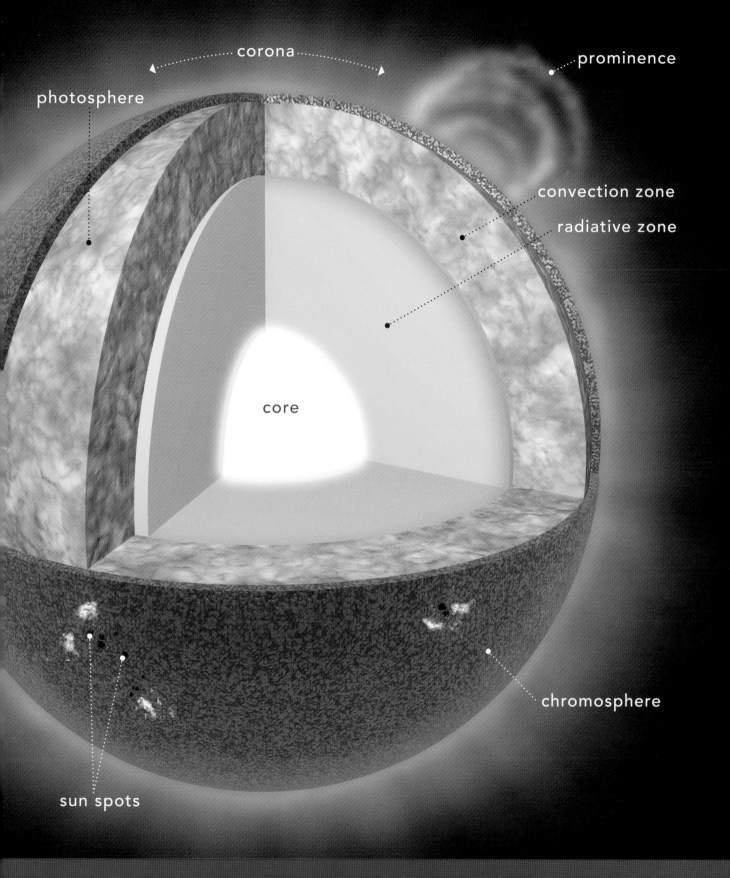

corona

prominence

photosphere

convection zone

radiative zone

core

chromosphere

sun spots

LOCATING THE SUN

—— **What you need** ——

A large square of cardboard,
a wooden stick, glue, a marker

What you do

Glue one end of the stick to the cardboard. Place the board somewhere flat where the sun shines on it. The stick should make a shadow. Mark on the board where the tip of the shadow ends. Repeat this every day for a week, and see how the sun "moves"!

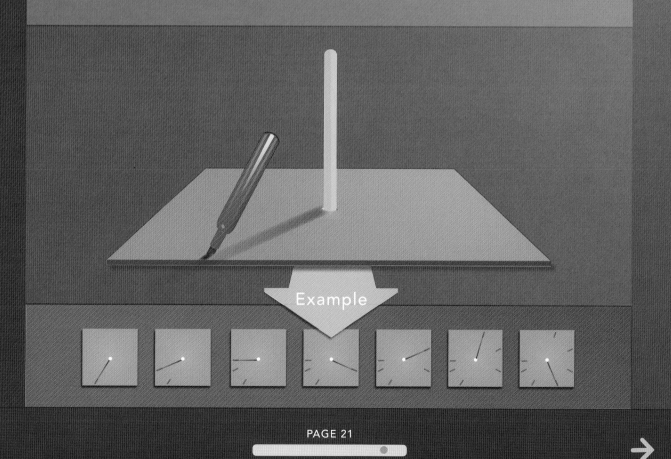

Example

GLOSSARY

	galaxy	a collection of stars held together by gravity
	gravity	the force that pulls objects toward each other
	planets	rounded objects that move around a star
	solar system	the sun, the planets, and their moons

READ MORE

Sexton, Colleen. *The Sun.*
Minneapolis: Bellwether Media, 2010.

Simon, Seymour. *The Sun.*
New York: Morrow, 1996.

WEBSITES

Astronomy Games for Kids
http://www.kidsastronomy.com/fun/index.htm
Play games to learn more about the sun and astronomy.

NASA's The Space Place
http://spaceplace.nasa.gov/menu/sun/
Find fun solar activities, and watch videos about the sun.

Note: Every effort has been made to ensure that the websites listed above are suitable for children, that they have educational value, and that they contain no inappropriate material. However, because of the nature of the Internet, it is impossible to guarantee that these sites will remain active indefinitely or that their contents will not be altered.

INDEX